WORLD ALMANAC®
LIBRARY OF THE
Middle East

GEOGRAPHY AND RESOURCES

of the Middle East

David Downing

Academic Consultant:
William Ochsenwald
Professor of History, Virginia Polytechnic Institute
and State University

WORLD ALMANAC® LIBRARY

Please visit our website at: www.garethstevens.com
For a free color catalog describing World Almanac® Library's list of high-quality books
and multimedia programs, call 1-800-848-2928 (USA) or 1-800-387-3178 (Canada).
World Almanac® Library's Fax: (414) 332-3567.

Library of Congress Cataloging-in-Publication Data

Downing, David, 1946-
    Geography and resources of the Middle East / David Downing.
       p. cm. — (World Almanac Library of the Middle East)
    Includes bibliographical references and index.
    ISBN-10: 0-8368-7334-3 — ISBN-13: 978-0-8368-7334-4 (lib. bdg.)
    ISBN-10: 0-8368-7341-6 — ISBN-13: 978-0-8368-7341-2 (softcover)
    1. Middle East—Geography—Juvenile literature. 2. Natural resources—
Middle East—Juvenile literature. 3. Middle East—Social life and customs—
Juvenile literature. I. Title. II. Series.
    DS44.96.D68   2006
    915.6—dc22   2006014029

First published in 2007 by
World Almanac® Library
A Member of the WRC Media Family of Companies
330 West Olive Street, Suite 100
Milwaukee, WI 53212, USA

Produced by Discovery Books
Editors: Geoff Barker, Amy Bauman, Paul Humphrey, and Sarah Jameson
Series designer: Sabine Beaupré
Designer and page production: Ian Winton
Photo researchers: Sarah Jameson and Rachel Tisdale
Maps and diagrams: Stefan Chabluk and Ian Winton
Academic Consultant: William Ochsenwald,
    Professor of History, Virginia Polytechnic Institute and
    State University
World Almanac® Library editorial direction: Mark J. Sachner
World Almanac® Library editor: Alan Wachtel
World Almanac® Library art direction: Tammy West
World Almanac® Library production: Jessica Morris

Photo credits: cover: Geopress/Stone/Getty Images; p. 5: Karim Sahib/AFP/Getty Images;
p. 6: Wendy Chan/Image Bank/Getty Images; p. 9: Ali Yussef/AFP/Getty Images; p. 10:
Glen Allison/Stone/Getty Images; p. 13: Hartmut Schwarzbach/Still Pictures; p. 14:
©Ed Kashi/CORBIS; p. 16: Jean-Leo Dugas/Still Pictures; p. 18: Detlev Klose/Still Pictures;
p. 21: Geopress/Stone/Getty Images; p. 22: Robert Mulder/Still Pictures; p. 25: ©Ed
Kashi/CORBIS; p. 27: James Strachan/Image Bank/Getty Images; p. 28: Atta Kenare/AFP/
Getty Images; p. 30: Marco Di Lauro/Getty Images; p. 33: Oliver Benn/Stone/Getty Images;
p. 35: ©Ed Kashi/CORBIS; p. 36: Behrouz Mehri/AFP/Getty Images; p. 38: Jocelyn Bain
Hogg/Still Pictures; p. 39: ©Ed Kashi/CORBIS; p. 40: Scott Nelson/Getty Images; p. 43:
Ben Edwards/Stone/Getty Images.

Printed in the United States of America

1 2 3 4 5 6 7 8 9 10 09 08 07 06

CONTENTS

Cover: *Cranes move an oil pipeline into position near Mareb in the desert interior of Yemen.*

The Middle East

The term *Middle East* has a long and complex history. It was originally used by the British in the nineteenth century to describe the area between the Near East (those lands gathered around the eastern end of the Mediterranean Sea) and Britain's empire in India. This area included Persia (later Iran), the **Mesopotamian provinces** of the **Ottoman Empire** (later Iraq), and the eastern half of Saudi Arabia. It was centered on the Persian Gulf.

In this series, the Middle East is taken to include the following fifteen countries: Libya and Egypt in north Africa,

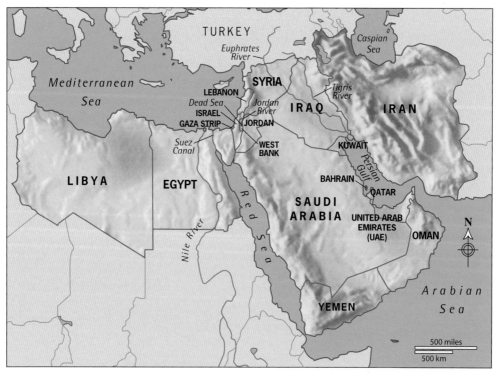

This map shows the fifteen countries of the Middle East that will be discussed in this book, as well as the West Bank and the Gaza Strip.

An Iraqi worker tends to pipes at an oil refinery in Basra, 1999. The war and subsequent unrest in Iraq (2003 onwards) have resulted in massive dislocation of the country's oil industry.

along with Israel, Lebanon, Syria, Jordan, Iraq, Iran, and the **Arabian peninsula** countries of Bahrain, Kuwait, Saudi Arabia, United Arab Emirates (UAE), Oman, Yemen, and Qatar. It also includes the disputed Arab Palestinian territories—the West Bank and Gaza Strip—which have had varying degrees of autonomy under Israeli occupation since 1967.

Why is this region important? Two reasons stand out. One, the Middle East was the original source of civilization, and the three great religions of Christianity, **Judaism**, and **Islam** all grew up there. The area includes Israel, the state of the Jewish people, and a significant proportion of the world's **Muslims**. Two, the Middle East has two-thirds of the fuel that keeps the rest of the world running—oil.

For these two reasons alone, the affairs of the Middle East— its peoples and resources, religions and politics, revolutions and wars—are of vital interest to everyone on the planet.

This book looks at the geography and resources of the Middle East. The physical environment is described, and the useful features that nature has provided for its inhabitants are explored. Changing ways of life and the region's borders are discussed. Finally, the geography and resources of the region's countries are examined in detail.

CHAPTER 1

Physical Geography

Location and Borders

The Middle East occupies the southwest corner of Asia and the northeast corner of Africa. To the north, the mountains of Turkey and the Russian Caucasus Mountains separate the Middle East from Europe. To the southwest, the Sahara Desert lies between the Middle East and tropical Africa, but there is no obvious border on the Mediterranean coast. Similarly, to the east and northeast, there is no clear dividing line between the desert **plateaus** of Iran and similar areas of central Asia, Afghanistan, and Pakistan.

Herdsmen drive their cattle across an empty road in the Dhofar region of Oman. This country experiences the hottest average temperatures in the Middle East.

Size and Climate

The Middle East is roughly the same size as the United States (excluding Alaska). The distance from western Libya to eastern Iran is around 3,000 miles (4,830 kilometers)—and from northern Iraq to Yemen's Indian Ocean coastline, around 1,500 miles (2,410 km).

In the United States and Europe, the most popular visual images of the Middle East are of sandy deserts, dusty cities, sluggish rivers, and dried-up riverbeds. All these things are widely found, but they are far from the whole story. The Middle East also has green coastal plains, grassy **steppes**, and high mountain ranges that receive regular snowfalls. Dryness, however, is the single most important feature of the region as a whole. A few fortunate areas—the Mediterranean coastlines of Israel and Lebanon for example—have an average yearly rainfall of more than 24 inches (610 millimeters). Libya, Egypt, Jordan, Iraq, most of Iran and the Arabian peninsula, all receive less than 8 inches (203 mm) of rain a year. January is generally the coldest month in the Middle East; July is the hottest. The northern areas and mountains have cold winters and hot summers; the southern areas experience warm winters and very hot summers. Temperatures drop sharply at night, especially in areas away from the coasts and high in the hills and mountains.

TEMPERATURE AND RAINFALL

Middle East locations	Coldest Month Average Temperature °F	Coldest Month Average Temperature °C	Hottest Month Average Temperature °F	Hottest Month Average Temperature °C	Annual Rainfall (inches)	Annual Rainfall (millimeters)
Manama (Bahrain)	66	19	97	36	5.2	132
Cairo (Egypt)	56	13	83	28	1.2	30
Tehran (Iran)	36	2	85	29	10	254
Baghdad (Iraq)	50	10	95	35	6	152
Tel Aviv (Israel)	62	17	86	30	31.6	803
Amman (Jordan)	46	8	77	25	13.4	340
Kuwait City (Kuwait)	56	13	99	37	5	127
Beirut (Lebanon)	55	13	81	27	35.7	907
Tripoli (Libya)	52	11	81	27	16	406
Muscat (Oman)	82	28	114	46	4	102
Doha (Qatar)	62	17	98	37	2.5	63.5
Riyadh (Saudi Arabia)	58	14	108	42	4	102
Damascus (Syria)	38	3	77	25	8.8	223
Dubai (UAE)	74	23	108	42	2.4	61
Aden (Yemen)	75	24	90	32	1.8	46

Source: The Statesman's Yearbook 2005 (Palgrave, Macmillan)

This table shows average temperatures and annual rainfall at selected locations in the Middle East.

Rivers and Vegetation

Much of the region's low rainfall is **evaporated** by the high temperatures, and a general shortage of surface freshwater is a constant problem. The Middle East has only four major rivers that flow throughout the year, and only one of these—the Jordan River—has its source in the Middle East. The Euphrates and Tigris Rivers, which flow through Iraq, rise, or begin, in the mountains of Turkey. The Nile, which is Egypt's only major water source, rises in Uganda and Ethiopia.

In the river valleys and coastal and mountain areas that receive significant rainfall, a wide variety of vegetation grows. Areas of both **coniferous** and **deciduous** forest are found in the Iranian and Lebanese mountains. The river plains are studded with trees, the most common of which is the date palm. Giant reeds flourish in these slow-moving rivers as they near the sea. Fruit trees, grapevines, and wheat grow widely on the coastal plains of Israel, Lebanon, and Syria. In the drier steppe regions, vegetation is limited to mostly shrubs and grasses.

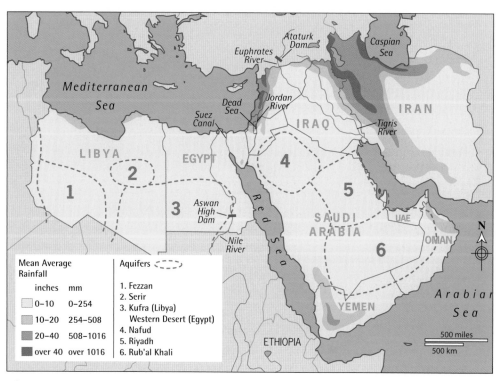

This map shows the major aquifers and areas of significant rainfall in the Middle East. The overall dryness of the region is apparent.

Cattle are herded across a channel of the Tigris River, close to the city of Baquba, northeast of Iraq's capital, Baghdad.

Extensive areas of sand desert cover Saudi Arabia, Libya, and Egypt, and equally wide areas of rock, stone, and gravel desert are found in these and other countries of the region. What little rain that falls comes in sudden storms, filling the dry channels (called **wadis**) with churning water for a few hours. By the following day, the water has either sunk beneath the surface or evaporated in the tremendous heat.

Aquifers

With few rivers and large areas of the region lacking significant rainfall, much of the Middle East is dependent on underground basins, or **aquifers**. There are two basic types. Shallow aquifers are fed by rainfall and general seepage. Sometimes these are under rivers or dry riverbeds; sometimes they are found far from an obvious water source. Aquifers under the United Arab Emirates, for example, are fed by underground channels carrying water from the mountains of Oman. Such aquifers can usually be reached by digging wells.

Deep aquifers are huge underground storage caverns in limestone or sandstone that filled with water thousands of years ago. Six major deep aquifers underlie most of Libya, Egypt, and Arabia, and contain around 38,000 cubic miles (158,380 cubic km) of water. These sources of water, which are reached by drilling, are likely to become increasingly important in future years.

CHAPTER 2

Resources of the Middle East

Each of the Middle East's geographical areas—its coastal plains, river valleys, steppes, mountains, and deserts—has resources that humans can use. Some of these resources, like the waters of the Nile, have been used for thousands of years. Others, like the vast reservoirs of oil deep below the sands of the Arabian peninsula, have only been put to use in the last century.

Agricultural Resources

Only small areas of the region possess the well-watered, **fertile soil** suitable for intensive crop growing. These areas include the Nile Delta in Egypt and the Euphrates-Tigris **floodplain** (both of which have rich **alluvial soils**), the western end of the **Fertile Crescent** and small areas of Yemen and Oman. Most of the region's higher ground is suitable for **pasture**, particularly in Iran,

Yemeni women in traditional dress lead their herd of goats. The palm trees in the background suggest that water is present nearby.

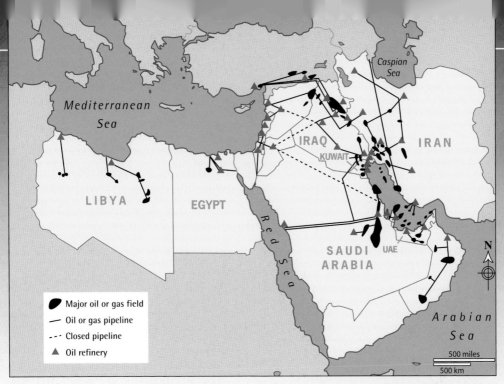

This map outlines the major oil fields, refineries, and pipelines of the Middle East. The 25 largest oil fields each contain more than 5 billion barrels of oil.

Iraq, and Yemen. Sheep, cattle, and goats are raised by farmers in the Middle East and chickens are kept almost everywhere.

The seas that border the Middle East have their share of fish, but Middle Eastern fishing fleets are small by world standards. Iran, Oman, and the United Arab Emirates are the main sea-fishers; Egypt catches more river fish than all of the region's other countries combined.

Even the deserts offer a few resources for survival. Underground sources of water can be reached by wells, and in many places there is enough vegetation to feed a few animals.

Mineral Resources

A wide variety of **nonfuel minerals** are found in the Middle East—sixty different types, for example, are found in Iran—but the true extent of the region's nonfuel mineral wealth is still unknown. **Fuel minerals**—oil and natural gas—are another matter. According to current estimates, Iran, Iraq, Kuwait, the United Arab Emirates, Saudi Arabia, and Libya together have slightly over two-thirds of the world's **proven reserves** of oil. The Middle East also contains more than one-third of the world's proven reserves of natural gas.

People

The resources of the Middle East include its more than 272 million people. The United States, by comparison, has a population of more than 295 million, occupying roughly the same land area. But much less of the Middle East than the United States is suitable for permanent settlement, and its people tend to be concentrated in small areas. The Nile Delta area, which is not much bigger than the state of Maryland, contains almost a quarter of the population of the Middle East.

When discussing the people of the Middle East, Americans and Europeans tend to think of Arabs and Jews. Ancestors of both have lived in the region for thousands of years. Today's Arabs are the result of intermixing between the original Arabian desert-dwellers and other **ethnic groups** like the original Egyptians. These people are now unified by centuries of common culture and the acceptance of Arabic as their common language. Many of the Jews who make up Israel's population come from families who immigrated to the area in the twentieth century.

Arabs account for about 70 percent of the Middle East's population; Jews make up about 2 percent. About 16 percent are ethnic Persians (or Iranians); another 4.5 percent are **Kurds**.

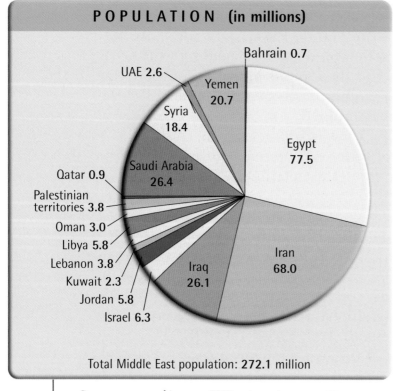

POPULATION (in millions)

Bahrain 0.7
UAE 2.6
Yemen 20.7
Syria 18.4
Egypt 77.5
Saudi Arabia 26.4
Qatar 0.9
Palestinian territories 3.8
Oman 3.0
Libya 5.8
Lebanon 3.8
Kuwait 2.3
Jordan 5.8
Israel 6.3
Iraq 26.1
Iran 68.0

Total Middle East population: **272.1 million**

Source: www.geohive.com (2005 estimates)

This pie chart shows the populations of countries in the Middle East. The importance of Egypt and Iran is obvious.

Making Money Out of Ruins

The Middle East was home to many of the world's ancient civilizations, which provides it with another potentially rich resource—the ruins that those civilizations left behind. The Egyptian, Persian, and Arab Empires all left physical traces of their existence, and Islamic architects and builders have created some of the most beautiful buildings on the planet. Most parts of the region have something to offer the tourist, from a peaceful cruise down the Nile River to adventure-trekking in the mountains of Yemen.

Guides on colorfully adorned camels wait beside one of Egypt's pyramids. They offer sight-seeing camel rides to tourists.

A Rising Population

The population of the Middle East roughly doubled in the last thirty years of the twentieth century. There were several reasons for this. While increasing access to modern medicine has meant people live longer, the desire for large families continued. This was particularly true in poorer areas, where children were often seen as extra pairs of hands for agricultural work.

Many Middle Eastern governments have tried to encourage smaller families. This is important, because the recent rise in population has already put a severe strain on food and water resources in the region's poorer countries.

CHAPTER 3

Life in the Middle East

Since ancient times there have been three basic ways of life in the Middle East—**nomadic** life, village life, and city life. All three lifestyles still exist today, but over the last century each has undergone dramatic changes. The balance between them has also changed.

In Syria's fertile Ghab valley, a Bedouin family grazes its sheep on the stubble of a harvested wheat field.

Three Traditional Ways of Life

In the Middle East, most **nomads** are **Bedouins**. Nomadic people have lived in the desert and semidesert areas of the region for thousands of years, moving their herds of sheep, goats, and camels in search of fresh pasture. They live in tents woven from animal hair and mostly eat what their animals provide—milk, cheese, and butter. They sometimes trade for rice, grain, and fruit with settled communities, but generally speaking their diet is monotonous and unbalanced. Few Bedouins live much beyond fifty years of age.

A settled agricultural lifestyle was born in the Nile and Euphrates-Tigris valleys around 6000 B.C., and village life has been an important part of the Middle East ever since. Until recently, the vast majority of the population lived and worked in villages, and around half of the people still do. These villages are found wherever there is rain or river water to support some sort of farming, whether crop or animal based. The villages themselves are built on the least fertile areas of ground, so as not to waste precious cropland. The mud-brick houses share narrow alleys and a few communal facilities.

Urban life came into being in the Middle East around 4000 B.C. Cities began as places where goods were exchanged and long-distance trade was organized. Cities such as Babylon in what is now Iraq and Memphis in what is now Egypt—though neither city exists today—were two early examples of important urban communities. The city of Damascus, the modern capital of Syria, grew up on the trade route between Iraq and the Mediterranean coast almost four thousand years ago.

As trade spread beyond the Middle East, the cities of the region became staging posts on trade routes—like the famous **Silk Road**—connecting China, the Middle East, and Europe. Between the eighth and thirteenth centuries, the spread of Islam and Arab power allowed cities like Cairo and Baghdad to become world leaders in science and culture. Like the villages of the Middle East, the cities were noted for their narrow streets, but the range of facilities they provided was the largest to be found on Earth. The markets of Middle Eastern cities boasted the widest range of goods and their hospitals and libraries offered the best medical care and books.

The Beginnings of Change

As a result of the breakup of the great Arab civilizations and the European development of sea routes to Asia, the great cities of the Middle East became global backwaters, pale copies of their former splendor. Between the thirteenth and nineteenth centuries, nomadic and village life continued with little change. Urban life largely stagnated.

Around the end of the nineteenth century, new life came to the Middle East. European countries showed renewed interest in the area. The Middle East lay along British and French communication routes with their Asian empires. The world's interest in the area grew stronger still when it became apparent, early in the twentieth century, that oil was the fuel of the future, and that the Middle East contained very large quantities of it under the ground.

Camels on the way to market in Misratha, Libya. The number of camels in the Middle East has—like the number of horses in the United States—shrunk since the introduction of the motor vehicle.

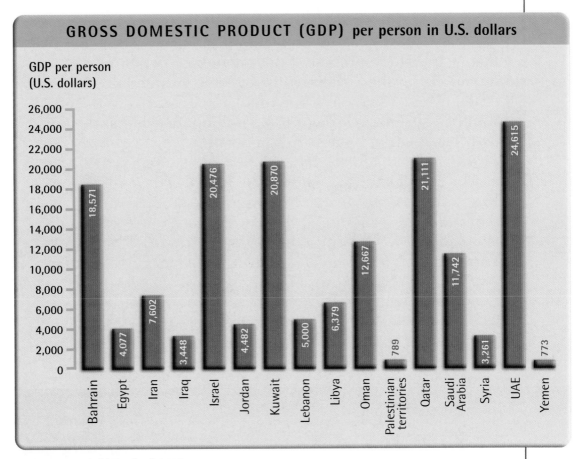

GROSS DOMESTIC PRODUCT (GDP) per person in U.S. dollars

GDP per person (U.S. dollars)

Country	GDP per person
Bahrain	18,571
Egypt	4,077
Iran	7,602
Iraq	3,448
Israel	20,476
Jordan	4,482
Kuwait	20,870
Lebanon	5,000
Libya	6,379
Oman	12,667
Palestinian territories	789
Qatar	21,111
Saudi Arabia	11,742
Syria	3,261
UAE	24,615
Yemen	773

Source: CIA World Factbook 2005

GDP or Gross Domestic Product is the sum total of what a country produces. So, roughly speaking, the higher the GDP per person, the richer the country is.

During and after World War I (1914–1918), Britain and France took action to protect their interests in the region. By the 1920s, most of the Middle East was under their control. This had important political consequences, but it also had a profound impact on Middle Eastern ways of life. The foreigners brought new agricultural and industrial techniques, new cultural ideas, modern Western medicine, and modern life.

A New Middle East

This process of modernization began slowly, but by the middle of the twentieth century, it was beginning to transform the region. Since the 1950s, then, the Middle East has seen enormous changes to all three traditional ways of life.

Nomadic life has declined. Some of the Bedouin traditional lands are now farmlands or oil fields. Some governments, like that in Iran, have pressured their country's Bedouin to settle in one place, where they can be better controlled. By the end of the twentieth century, the numbers of nomads in the Middle East had shrunk to around three million, which is little more than 1 percent of the region's population.

Village life has also changed. People live longer thanks to modern medicine, and educational facilities have improved. In some areas, new technologies have allowed expansion of the land used for farming. Modern media, such as radio and television, now reach into the farthest corners of the Middle East, reducing isolation and offering villagers glimpses of city life. However, longer lives also mean more mouths to feed, and the promise of the cities has tempted many young people away from their villages. Family ties generally remain strong, however, and most of those who move send money home to the villages.

Sheik Said Road in Dubai (United Arab Emirates) offers a striking demonstration of how oil profits can transform a desert.

Getting Around

The Middle East has a poorly developed **transportation infrastructure**. Its relatively few railroads were constructed in **colonial** times. They were usually built to connect the interior of countries with their most important port, allowing the transportation of **exports** in one direction and the swift arrival of colonial armies in the other. Major routes connecting parts of the Middle East with each other, like the Fertile Crescent route from Syria to Iraq, were not given a rail link.

Apart from the Nile, Tigris, and Euphrates rivers, no Middle Eastern rivers are capable of carrying significant traffic and there is little coastal shipping. In most populated parts of the region, such as the Mediterranean and Gulf coastal strips, a network of modern roads exists, but much of the region's desert interior is served only by rough railroad tracks. Building modern roads in the desert is expensive and not always worthwhile, because many of them will be washed away by flash floods.

The region is well-served by airports and flight routes. In previous centuries, thousands of pilgrims arrived at Mecca—the Saudi Arabian city that is the center of the Muslim faith—after months of overland travel; today travelers can step off the plane at the King Abdulaziz International airport in Jeddah and ride the last 40 miles (64 km) in a minibus.

Urban changes

The third way of life, urban life, has expanded enormously. At the end of the nineteenth century, less than 10 percent of Middle Easterners lived in towns, but now, in the early twenty-first century, that figure has grown to more than 50 percent. Some cities, such as Cairo (ten million inhabitants) and Tehran (eleven million inhabitants), are huge by any standards. As a city's population grows, the look of the city changes. New cities have been built—and some old cities rebuilt—with wider roads and modern buildings. Other old cities, like Cairo, have built new towns of modern skyscrapers and suburban villas alongside the old town of twisting alleys and covered markets.

The Importance of Oil

The single, most important factor influencing Middle Eastern ways of life in the last century has been the development of its most famous resource: oil. Oil has made the region important to the rest of the world. It has played an important role in alliances and power politics in the region. It has brought enormous wealth to many individuals and countries in the region.

Among the oil fields, new towns, roads, and shipping terminals have sprung into existence. Pipelines extend across the desert, and flames of burning gas light the night sky. Oil has divided the Middle East between those countries with big reserves of oil and those with little or none. Saudi Arabia, Iraq, Iran, Kuwait, Qatar, the UAE, and Libya fall into the first category; the rest make up the second.

The oil-rich states have used a significant portion of their newfound wealth to transform themselves. They spend money on making semidesert land suitable for agriculture, or on developing new industries. Saudi Arabia, for example, has

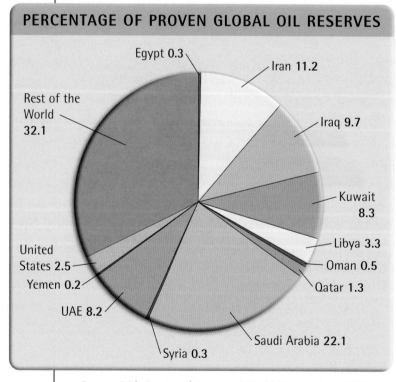

PERCENTAGE OF PROVEN GLOBAL OIL RESERVES

Egypt 0.3
Iran 11.2
Iraq 9.7
Rest of the World 32.1
Kuwait 8.3
Libya 3.3
Oman 0.5
United States 2.5
Yemen 0.2
Qatar 1.3
UAE 8.2
Saudi Arabia 22.1
Syria 0.3

This pie chart shows the importance of the Middle East in terms of global oil reserves.

Source: BP's Statistical Review of World Energy, June 2005
www.geohive.com

Cranes move an oil pipeline into position near Mareb in the desert interior of Yemen.

greatly expanded its wheat production. Bahrain has used the profits from its now exhausted oil wells to develop a **financial services** industry. Health and education facilities have also been improved.

The oil-poor states, however, have one thing that the Arabian oil-rich states do not have—high populations and a plentiful supply of skilled labor. Millions of Egyptians, Palestinians, Syrians, Jordanians, and Yemenis have gone to earn their living in the oil-rich states. The money they send home to their families has become crucial to the economies of the oil-poor states.

Control of Oil

"The Soviet Union is now attempting to consolidate a strategic position...that poses a grave threat to the free movement of Middle East oil...Let our position be absolutely clear: An attempt by any outside force to gain control of the Persian Gulf region will be regarded as an assault on the vital interests of the United States of America, and such an assault will be repelled by any means necessary, including military force."

President Jimmy Carter announces, in his 1980 State of the Union address, that the U.S. will use force to ensure the uninterrupted flow of Middle Eastern oil to the West.

CHAPTER 4

Borders of the Middle East

Problematic Borders

Before World War I, the Middle East had few borders. Today's Jordan, Syria, Israel, the Palestinian territories, and Iraq were all part of the Ottoman Empire, along with poorly defined strips of territory on the Persian Gulf and Red Sea coasts of the Arabian peninsula. A mountain border separated the Ottoman Empire from Iran; the Sinai Desert lay between Ottoman **Palestine** and British-controlled Egypt. Italy occupied Libya.

After World War I, Palestine, Transjordan (now Jordan), and Iraq became British **mandate territories**, and Syria and Lebanon became French mandate territories. Straight lines were drawn across the semidesert, dividing the region between them.

The controversial Israel security barrier winds through the outskirts of Jerusalem, dividing the suburb of Ophel (right) from the Palestinian village of Silwan (left).

The Borders of Iraq

The borders of Iraq offer examples of most of the problems
affecting Middle Eastern borders. The country's mountain
borders with Iran and Turkey, though undisputed, run right
through Kurdistan (the area occupied by the Kurds) and are
ignored by those who live on either side of them. The original
river border with Iran on the Shatt al Arab, which followed the
Iranian bank rather than the more-usual center of the river, was
imposed by the British in 1913, and has been disputed ever
since. The land border with Kuwait passes right through the
huge Rumeilah oil field, and the land border with Saudi Arabia—
a series of straight lines through the desert—cuts across the
traditional routes of nomadic tribespeople.

The French carved Lebanon out of Syria to give the pro-
European **Maronite Christians** a majority state of their own.
The Kurds were divided between four countries. The British
demanded that the Kurdish Mosul region be included in their
mandate territory of Iraq, because it contained important oil fields.
In the early twenty-first century, some neighboring countries
have still not reached agreement on the borders between them.
Saudi Arabia has long been in border disputes with most of its
Arabian neighbors. The Shatt al Arab River boundary between
Iraq and Iran has also been a constant source of friction. And,
finally, conflict persists between Israel and the Palestinian
Arabs, including contoversy over the borders of a possible
Palestinian state.

Open Borders

Few of the Middle East's borders represent a clean break
between geographic regions or different ethnic groups. Many
of them run through remote mountains or desert, all of which
makes them easy to cross and hard to police.

The Middle East has always acted as a gateway between Asia
and Europe. In past times, armies rampaged across the region
and traders passed through carrying silks and spices. Today,
however, the overland travelers who cross these borders are
often drug dealers or terrorists. The borders of the Middle East
are poorly placed to stop either.

Borders, Oil, and Water

When most of the Middle East's borders were drawn up, the search for underground oil had only just begun. Not surprisingly, many borders cut across the oil fields that were found to lie below the surface. Equally unsurprisingly, this has led to conflict. Disputes over **maritime** borders in the Persian Gulf have been about the ownership of oil and gas beneath the ocean floor.

Where water is concerned, two kinds of problems erupt. The first problem arises from the fact that much of the region's water falls to Earth outside the region. Egypt and Iraq depend on the Nile and Tigris-Euphrates rivers respectively, and the headwaters, or origins, of these vital rivers are beyond their borders and their reach. If Turkey or Ethiopia were to decide to take more water for themselves, the downstream states could do little more than hope that international pressure would insist on a fair division.

A similar problem actually occurred in the region in the 1960s. Syria and Jordan expressed their hostility toward Israel by threatening to reduce the flow of the Jordan River before it reached Israel. The resulting dispute played a part in causing the Arab–Israeli War of 1967.

The second major problem concerns water resources located within the region. These disputes can be over surface water, like the long-running dispute between Oman and the

The Water Crisis

"At the moment, I project the scarcity of water within 5 years...I can promise that if there is not sufficient water in our region, if there is scarcity of water, if people remain thirsty for water, then we shall doubtless face war..."

Meir Ben Meir, Israel's Water Commissioner talking about possible conflict over water between Israel, the Palestinians, Jordan, and Syria.

"They've got to change their crops, cut down on citrus, cut down on rice...You grow rice and cotton in the desert. They are the most water-consuming crops of all. If they do that, then really we have a chance to save a lot in the consumption of water."

Nabil Sha'ath, the Palestinian Authority's Minister of Planning and International Co-operation, commenting on Israeli agricultural practices.

(from Paul Welsh, *Water Conflict in Middle East*, BBC News Online June 2, 2000.)

These Syrian Bedouins are using modern technology to dig a well for water in the desert. The water these wells provide for their herds is encouraging the once nomadic Bedouins to settle beside them.

United Arab Emirates over the Buraimi **Oasis**. Or they can be over how much water each state takes from the aquifers that lie beneath the region, which bear no relation to political boundaries on the surface. The division of the water beneath the historical region of Palestine is one of the many issues complicating a division of the territory into two countries.

The Ataturk Dam

The Euphrates River rises in Turkey before flowing through Syria and Iraq. In the 1980s, the Turkish government decided to build the huge Ataturk Dam on the river. The intent of this project, called the Southeastern Anatolia (or GAP) Project, is to generate **hydroelectric power** and create large-scale **irrigation** facilities in southeastern Turkey. While water used to generate electricity is not lost to the river, the lake created behind the dam results in a large loss of water through evaporation. It seems inevitable that the still-to-be-completed GAP Project will result in a permanent reduction of the water reaching Syria and Iraq. Syria also has plans to use more of the river's water, further reducing the amount that will flow through Iraq. Not surprisingly, the Iraqis fear that these plans will leave insufficient water for their faucets and irrigation channels.

Countries of the Middle East

This chapter will explore each of the countries and other territories of the Middle East:

Bahrain consists of one large and several very small islands in the Persian Gulf. The country's main island is linked to the Arabian mainland by a seventeen-mile (27-km) **causeway**. Its climate is hot and humid, but there is hardly any rainfall. The country's reserves of oil are now almost exhausted, but earlier revenue was used to set up aluminum-smelting and shipbuilding industries and to launch the country as an important trading and financial center. The climate and soil severely limit the amount of land available for agriculture. Fruit, dates, and alfalfa are the main crops. The capital, Manama, is a small, modern town on the northeast coast of Bahrain island. The population of the country is around 650,000.

Egypt occupies the northeast corner of Africa, where that continent joins Asia. It is a large country (roughly the size of the states of Texas and New Mexico combined), but the population of around 77 million (over one quarter of the entire Middle East population) live in a small portion of that area. Because desert covers most of the country, life revolves around the Nile—the world's longest river and Egypt's only significant source of water. In the 1960s, construction began on the Aswan High Dam in southern Egypt to regulate the river's flow and produce hydroelectric power. Egypt's man-made Suez Canal connects the Red and Mediterranean seas.

Egypt's climate is mostly hot and dry, though the northern coast and fertile Nile Delta region do receive some rainfall.

Rice, corn, wheat, barley, fruit (particularly oranges), cotton, and sugar cane are grown in the Nile Delta and Valley. Despite intensive use of all its available agricultural land, Egypt cannot produce enough food for its own population.

Egypt has some oil, and has developed oil-refining and chemical industries. Textiles, cigarettes, soap, and processed food are other important industries. The remains of Egypt's glorious past—the pyramids near Cairo, the Valley of the Kings at Luxor, and many other sites—offer great potential for tourism, but terrorist attacks on tourists in the 1990s and early 21st century—and the fear of others in the future—has limited the number of visitors in recent years. The capital of Cairo is a huge city of ten million people, sited on the Nile.

This is a panoramic view of old Cairo, Egypt. Its small, twisting streets are in marked contrast to the broad avenues of the city's more modern areas.

Iran, which lies between the Caspian Sea on one side and the Persian Gulf and Indian Ocean on the other, is the easternmost country of the Middle East. Its population of around 68 million is less than Egypt's, but Iran is much larger. From the knot of mountains in the northwestern corner, two mountain ranges—the Elburz and Zagros—head east and southeast respectively, flanking the wide expanse of high plateau that occupies most of the country. The northeastern and eastern parts of this plateau are large salt deserts, the Dasht-e-Lut and Dasht-e-Kavir. There are strips of coastal plain on the Caspian Sea in the north and the Persian Gulf/Indian Ocean in the south.

These Kurdish workers are making bricks in Pakdasht, a small Iranian town about 30 miles (50 km) southeast of the capital Tehran.

A Patchwork of Peoples

The Middle East is often seen as an Arab Islamic sea, with Israel representing a small Jewish island at its heart. It is, however, much more complicated than that. A vast majority of Middle Easterners are Arabs, and a vast majority of them are Muslims. Iranians, although they are mostly Muslims, are not Arabs. Many Arabs, particularly in Lebanon, the Palestinian territories, and Egypt, are Christians. And many countries include small but significant minorities, such as the Shi'a Alawites in Syria, the Druze sect in Lebanon, the Christian Copts in Egypt, the Assyrians in Iraq, and the Zoroastrians in Iran.

Iran's climate varies from region to region; it is wetter and cooler toward the northwest, and hotter and drier toward the south and east. Summers are hot everywhere, but winters in the north are cold. Wheat, oats, and barley are grown in the valleys of the northwest; rice, cotton, grapes, and tobacco in those of the southwest. Tea, citrus fruit, and sugarcane are cultivated on the subtropical Caspian coast. Large areas of the hills and mountains provide pasture for Iran's 55 million sheep and 26 million goats.

Iran has significant mineral wealth, and much of it is still unexploited. Oil, however, dominates the economy, and Iran has around 11 percent of proven global reserves. The country also has significant textile and machinery industries, but earlier attempts to accelerate industrialization were halted by the Islamic Revolution of 1979 and, after that, the Iran-Iraq War of 1980–1988.

Treasures like the mosque at Isfahan and the ancient Persian capital of Persepolis have great tourist potential, but government hostility toward the West has deterred many Westerners from visiting. The capital of Tehran is a large bustling city of 11 million inhabitants near the southern slopes of the snow-covered Elburz Mountains. Tabriz in the northwest, Mashhad in the northeast, and Shiraz in the south are the country's other major cities.

An Iraqi fisherman casts his net into the Tigris River. One of Iraq's two great rivers, the Tigris is 1,150 miles (1,800 km) long. It joins the Euphrates, for the final stretch down to the Persian Gulf.

Iraq is centered on the floodplain of the Tigris and Euphrates rivers—the area that was once called Mesopotamia. This area is surrounded to the north and northwest by dry hills and mountains and gives way in the south and east to a desert of gravel and rock. The country is about the size of California, and its population of about 26 million is divided between three main groups—Arab Shi'a Muslims, Arab Sunni Muslims, and Kurdish Sunni Muslims.

Both the Tigris and Euphrates rivers rise in Turkey and flow southeastward through Iraq. One hundred and fifty miles (240 km) from the Persian Gulf, they merge to form the Shatt al Arab. The vast plain that surrounds these rivers has been irrigated for thousands of years, but the areas of rich agricultural soil are limited by high levels of salt. Only about 12 percent of Iraq's land can be farmed. Grains and tobacco are grown in the north; dates, cotton, corn, and rice are raised in the south.

Iraq has about 10 percent of proven global oil reserves. After Saddam Hussein took power in 1979, his Ba'ath regime increased the country's industrial capacity, but the political events of the last twenty-five years—the Iran-Iraq War (1980–1988), the Gulf War (1991), sanctions imposed by the United Nations (from 1991 until after the 2003 invasion), the Iraq War and its violent aftermath (since 2003)—have reduced much of the country to virtual ruin. Industry and agriculture are struggling to recover, and tourism, at present, is nonexistent.

The capital city of Baghdad lies on the Tigris some 400 miles (645 km) from the sea. A once-thriving city of five million people, it is now a virtual war zone. Other important cities are Basra in the south, the Shi'a holy cities of Karbala and Najaf on the Euphrates, and the northern cities of Mosul and Kirkuk, both of which have large Kurdish populations.

Kurdistan

Kurdistan is the name given to the region occupied by the Kurds. It consists of the northwestern corner of Iran, the northeastern corner of Iraq, the southeastern corner of Turkey, and a small slice of Syria. A country of hills, plateaus, and mountains, Kurdistan has no access to the sea, but it does have water: the Euphrates flows through it, and the Tigris rises in it. The Kurds have had their own culture and language for nearly 3,000 years. Their traditional way of life is **pastoral**, but both Turkish and Iraqi Kurdistan contain important oil fields. Turkey's Ataturk Dam and the GAP Project (for irrigation) are also situated in Kurdistan. In fact, more Kurds live in Turkey than in the Middle East. Originally a nomadic people, they are generally considered the most numerous people in the world without a state of their own.

Israel is a small country on the eastern shore of the Mediterranean Sea. Created in 1947 by the United Nations in part of the British mandate territory of Palestine, it came to control the whole former mandate territory as a result of the Arab-Israeli wars. In 2005, Israel withdrew from part of the occupied territories. The possibility exists that it will withdraw from more territory and that an independent Palestinian state will be founded. The current population is around 6.3 million.

Moving east from the Mediterranean, a narrow coastal plain gives way to a region of dry hills, which drop away to the valley of the Jordan River. The river itself, which marks Israel's eastern border, flows south into the Dead Sea, a body of exceptionally salty water. A large desert—the Negev—occupies the country's southern third. Most of Israel's rain falls in the north and extreme west, but extensive irrigation work has made agriculture possible in other areas as well. Israel grows enough food for its own population and also exports a considerable volume of fruit and vegetables. Israel has significant reserves of copper and phosphates.

With a highly skilled and educated workforce, Israel has developed high-tech electronic, **biotech**, **armaments**, and software industries. It also has chemical, cement, glass, and paper industries. Modern highways connect the sophisticated cities

LITERACY RATES (percentage of population)	
Bahrain	89.1
Egypt	57.7
Iran	79.4
Iraq	40.4
Israel	95.4
Jordan	91.4
Kuwait	83.5
Lebanon	87.4
Libya	82.6
Oman	75.8
Palestinian territories	no data available
Qatar	82.5
Saudi Arabia	78.8
Syria	76.9
UAE	77.9
Yemen	50.2

Source: 2006 World Almanac® and Book of Facts.

This table shows Middle Eastern literacy rates. The low figures for Yemen and Egypt reflect large rural populations that still lack access to reasonable educational facilities.

Orthodox Jews pray at the Western (Wailing) Wall in Jerusalem, the city which both Israelis and the Palestinians claim as their capital.

of Tel Aviv, Haifa, and west Jerusalem. East Jerusalem, a city sacred to three religions — Christianity, Judaism, and Islam — has immense tourist potential. The success of that industry, however, will depend on whether a peaceful settlement can finally be reached with the Palestinians.

Jordan comprises the eastern side of the Jordan River valley and a large area of desert plateau adjoining Iraq and Saudi Arabia. There is a short 16-mile (26-km) coastline on the Red Sea. The population of around 5.8 million is of mixed Bedouin-Palestinian origin and is high for the available resources. The country's climate is hot and dry, and the area suitable for agriculture is very limited. Wheat, barley, olives, and citrus fruits are grown in the Jordan River valley, and sheep and goats are kept in the hills immediately to the east. The country exports phosphates but has no oil. It also has textile, cement, and cigarette industries. The ruins of ancient Petra and the scenic splendor of the Wadi Rumm — where much of the movie *Lawrence of Arabia* was filmed — bring in much-needed tourist revenue.

The Founding of Israel

"It is the natural right of the Jewish people to lead, as do all other nations, an independent existence in their sovereign State... Accordingly we, the members of the National Council representing the Jewish people in Palestine...hereby proclaim the establishment of the Jewish State in Palestine, to be called Medinath Yisrael (the State of Israel)."

From the State of Israel Declaration of Independence, May 14, 1948.

Increasing the Water Supply

Seawater is not fit for drinking or use in the cultivation of crops. Once the salt is removed, however, it can be used for both. The acute shortage of freshwater that affects many Middle Eastern countries has led some of them to invest large sums of money in **desalination** (de-salting) plants. The region now has around two-thirds of the world's desalination capacity.

Desalination plants are very expensive to build and operate, so almost all of them are found in the oil-rich Persian Gulf states and Israel. There are, however, drawbacks to relying too heavily on this method of creating freshwater. First, small countries with only one or two plants can have their water supply cut off by terrorist or military attack. Second, because, the desalination process uses a lot of energy, it contributes to global warming.

Another way of increasing the freshwater supply is by recycling wastewater. It is estimated that Israel now reuses around 80 percent of its water, and Syria, Jordan, and some of the Gulf states are also increasing their water-recycling capacity.

Kuwait is a small desert country at the head of the Persian Gulf, sandwiched between Iraq and Saudi Arabia. The country has no mountains, natural lakes, or permanent rivers. Desert plains gently rise from the coastline. The climate of the country is very hot in summer, cool in winter, and dry all year round. Kuwait has over 8 percent of the world's proven reserves of oil and most of the country's 2.3 million inhabitants make their living, directly or indirectly, from this important resource. Oil-refining and chemical industries have been developed. The capital of the country is Kuwait City. Lying on the southern side of a huge bay, it is an increasingly important financial center.

Lebanon is a small country on the east Mediterranean coast between Israel and Syria. It is about 135 miles (217 km) long and 30–50 miles (48–80 km) wide. From east to west, it consists of four basic strips: a coastal plain, the Lebanon Mountains, the Beka'a Valley, and the Anti-Lebanon Mountains. The population of around 3.8 million is mixed, containing several Christian and several Muslim communities.

Lebanon has a Mediterranean climate with plentiful rainfall and it is the only country in the Middle East without any desert. Citrus fruit, vegetables, tobacco, grapes, silkworms, and grains are grown on the well-watered coastal plain and also in the slightly drier Beka'a Valley.

Before the sixteen-year civil war (1975–1991) Lebanon in general—and the capital, Beirut, in particular—had a wide range of successful trading, manufacturing, and tourist industries. Its economic activities are now slowly recovering. Beirut, which lies on the Mediterranean coast, is home to around 1.5 million people, or 40 percent of the country's population. The only other city of any size is Tripoli, in the north.

Officials of the Ministry of Public Works in Kuwait inspect pipelines that feed salt water into a desalination plant where it is purified into drinking water. The Middle East's need for such plants is likely to grow in future years.

Libya is the North African country that lies immediately to the west of Egypt. It is the second largest country in the Middle East, but only the narrow coastal strip and a few scattered oases are suitable for permanent settlement. Desert plains, plateaus, and mountains make up most of the country. Winter rain is plentiful enough to grow grains in parts of the coastal strip, but water in general is in short supply.

Happy Libyans celebrate the opening of the Salluq Reservoir, part of the Great Man-Made River Project. Seventy percent of the water delivered by the project is to be used for agriculture.

Climate Change

According to many scientists, global temperatures are rising, and this will result in a shift of existing climatic patterns. It is too early to say what this will mean for the Middle East, but a region already prone to climatic extremes may be seriously affected. The general prediction is that the region will experience more rain in the north and less in the south. While this change could be good for Syria and Iran, it could devastate North Africa and the Arabian peninsula. Reduced rainfall in these latter areas could turn a water shortage into a water famine and make an increasing number of areas unable to sustain human life.

The Great Man-Made River—one of the largest projects of its type in the world—has been built to bring water from several desert oases to the coastal region of Libya, where the majority of the population lives. Begun in 1984, the "river" runs underground for hundreds of miles through a network of pipes. This hugely expensive project has been financed by the country's oil wealth —the country has around 3 percent of proven global reserves. Iron and steel, along with chemical, and aluminum industries are also growing, but Libya's economic development has been hindered by international disapproval of Colonel Muammar Gaddafi's government. The capital city of Tripoli, founded by the Phoenicians in the seventh century B.C., lies on the coast.

Oman occupies the southeastern corner of the Arabian peninsula. Coastal plains to the north and south are divided by mountains, and the country's interior is desert. The climate is hot in winter and exceptionally hot in summer. The agricultural sector is quite small, but the northern coastal strip is famous for its dates. Around Salalah in the south, where the Indian Ocean **monsoon rains** create a lush **semitropical** environment, bananas and sugarcane are grown. Oil and gas, however, provide more than 75 percent of country's exports. Oil-refining, copper-smelting, and cement are its other major industries. The capital of Oman, Muscat, is located on the north coast.

Territories held by the **Palestinian National Authority** include those areas of the British mandate of Palestine that have not been internationally recognized as part of Israel. Two pieces of territory are involved. One is the Gaza Strip, a section of dry Mediterranean coastal plain roughly 25 miles (40 km) long and 6 miles (10 km) wide. The other is the West Bank, a region of mostly dry hills to the west of the Jordan River, roughly 100 miles (160 km) long and 30 miles (48 km) wide. Israel's occupation of the Gaza Strip ended in the summer of 2005, but access to the outside world is still severely restricted. The West Bank (which includes East Jerusalem) remains under Israeli occupation.

A Palestinian at work in an olive grove on the occupied West Bank. Olive trees can grow in very dry climates, provided there is some irrigation.

Neither piece of territory is particularly favorable for agriculture, and much of the available water is used by Israeli settlements. Wheat and olives are the principal crops on the West Bank, but the area has no oil or mineral resources. This fact, accompanied by long years of occupation and upheaval, has prevented the growth of any significant industrial development. If the regions of Gaza and the West Bank are ever to flourish, the Palestinians and the Israelis need to end their conflict. Then, with substantial international help, Palestine could develop its tourist potential, particularly if a new Palestinian state would include shared or sole sovereignty over Jerusalem's Old City.

Qatar occupies a 100-mile (160-km) long, flat desert peninsula jutting into the Persian Gulf. The climate is hot and dry, and the small agricultural sector

Palestinian farmers clear away unwanted irrigation pipes. There is no water to flow through them here.

relies on expensive irrigation. A majority of Qatar's 900,000 people are **immigrant workers**, drawn by the oil and service industries. Qatar has considerable oil reserves, and the third-highest proven reserves of natural gas in the world. Other industries include fertilizers, cement, steel, and oil-refining. The capital, Doha, is on the east coast.

On the Move

Over the last half century, the Middle East has seen enormous transfers of population. Some movements, such as that of Palestinian Arabs as a result of the 1947–1948 conflict, have been at least partly forced. Most movements of population, however, have been voluntary. Huge numbers of Middle Easterners have left their villages for the brighter lights and better opportunities of the cities of their own country. Equally huge numbers have left the oil-poor countries for the oil-rich countries, where work has usually been easier to find and better paid.

Saudi Arabia is the largest state in the Middle East. It comprises the vast interior of the Arabian peninsula, with coastlines on the Red Sea (about 1,000 miles/1,600 km) and Persian Gulf (350 miles/560 km). A chain of mountains runs behind the narrow Red Sea coastal plain. Beyond these, desert plateaus slope gently down toward a desert plain. The famous sand desert of the Rub al-Khali, the so-called Empty Quarter, is found in the far southeast. On the Red Sea coastal plain, there is some seasonal rain, but elsewhere the climate is hot, dry, and often windy. Dates and cereals have long been grown on the Red Sea coastal plain, but in recent years, huge investments in irrigation and livestock have seen an expansion

Helpers scramble for safety as racing camels and their riders wait at the start of a race. Camel racing has always been a pastime of the Bedouins, but during the last 20 years or so it has become a popular sport in the Arabian peninsula.

Camels

Nothing is more symbolic of the traditional Middle East than the camel, and the camel's role in the modern Middle East offers a striking picture of how much life in the region has changed in recent years. The camel's most useful quality for humans was its remarkable ability to survive for long periods without water. For thousands of years, Middle Easterners have used this animal to carry themselves and their goods on the long, dry journeys between cities and countries. In the twentieth century, however, camels largely lost their role in transportation. Cars and trucks became the method of choice for both personal and business transportation needs, and even desert nomads were as likely to use a Toyota pickup as a camel. Because of this, the camel's two major uses in today's Middle East are as a source of meat for special feast days and as racing animals for entertainment. Today, camels are found in large numbers only in Saudi Arabia.

of the land used for farming, and Saudi Arabia is now self-sufficient in wheat, potatoes, eggs, and dairy produce.

These agricultural investments were made possible by the country's huge oil revenues. Saudi Arabia, with a population of about 26 million people, has over 22 percent of the world's proven oil reserves. Oil-refining, chemical, steel, and fertilizer industries have sprung up among the oil fields, which are situated beneath the eastern desert plains and the Persian Gulf coast. The government's rigid application of **Islamic laws and customs** (which address topics as varied as the separation of the sexes and the banning of alcohol) make the country unsuitable for most Western tourists, but the millions of foreign Muslims who visit the holy city of Mecca generate significant income for the country.

The capital, Riyadh, is in the center of the country. Although the cities in the oil region are mostly new and modern, those in the west, such as Mecca, Medina, and the port city of Jeddah, retain at least some of their traditional appearance.

Syria is the northwestern outpost of the Arab world. Like Lebanon, it has a Mediterranean coastal plain and parallel mountain ranges, but most of the country is semidesert steppe and desert plateaus. The Euphrates River cuts across the northeast third of the country on its way from Turkey to Iraq. Most of the 18.4 million inhabitants live in the quarter of the country that is suitable for agriculture. Grapes, citrus fruits, vegetables, and tobacco are grown on the coastal plain; cotton and wheat are the crops of the inland steppe. Sheep and goats are widely reared. Syria has some oil and significant deposits of phosphates, salt, and **gypsum**. Textiles, chemicals, leather, woolen goods, cement, and food processing are the main industries. The government has encouraged tourism, but there is still the potential for attracting many more tourists. The capital, Damascus, the oldest major city in the world, is part modern and part traditional. Other important cities, all of which have a long history, are Aleppo, Homs, and Hama.

The **United Arab Emirates** (UAE) lie on the eastern coast of the Arabian peninsula, with coastlines on the Persian Gulf and the Gulf of Oman. The state was formed in 1971–1972 by merging seven **emirates**—Abu Dhabi, Dubai, Sharjah, Ajman, Umm al-Qaywayn, Ra's al-Khaymah, and Fujayrah. The current population is around 2.6 million. Most of the land is sandy desert plain, but mountains rise in the east. Rainfall is generally negligible, but it is sufficient enough in Ra's al-Khaymah and Fujayrah to support some crops. Oil, however, is one of the country's main resources. Abu Dhabi has large reserves, Dubai and Sharjah have smaller reserves, but together the UAE holds over 8 percent of proven global reserves. Cement and aluminum-smelting industries also contribute to the country's economy, and the city of Dubai has become a major trading center and tourist destination.

The recently-unified (1990) state of **Yemen** occupies the southwestern corner of the Arabian peninsula. Narrow plains on the Red Sea and the Indian Ocean coastlines are backed by high mountains in the country's west and southwest. In the south, the Wadi Masilah River provides seasonal water for the irrigation systems of the Hadhramawt region. The country's interior is desert. The summers are extremely hot, but rainfall

These mud-brick skyscrapers are in the city of Shibam in Yemen's Hadhramawt region. Shibam is often called "Manhattan in the desert."

in the hills allows farmers to grow cotton, coffee, fruit, and vegetables. Wheat, barley, **sorghum**, and cotton are grown in the Hadhramawt. Despite this, Yemen does not have enough farmland to feed its 20.7 million people and, in recent years, poor world food prices have led more and more farmers to grow *khat*. The leaves of this shrub, when chewed, are a mild drug. The country also has some oil but hardly any industry. Many of its people work as immigrant laborers in the oil-rich states. Yemen's capital, Sana'a, is high in the mountains. Aden, the former capital of South Yemen, was a British naval base until 1968. The Hadhramawt is famous for its villages of mud-brick "skyscrapers."

TIME LINE

Ninth millenium B.C. World's first farms developed in the Fertile Crescent.

Sixth millenium B.C. Settled agricultural lifestyle begins in Nile and Euphrates-Tigris valleys.

Fourth millenium B.C. Urban life comes into being in the Middle East.

Ca. 500 B.C. Nomadic Bedouin settle in Jordan and build city of Petra, one of the wonders of the ancient world.

A.D. 700–1200 Islam and Arab power spreads over the region. Cities of Cairo and Baghdad flourish.

762 Baghdad is founded and becomes one of the world's great trading cities.

1869 Suez Canal opens.

1908 Oil discovered in Iran.

1920s Most of Middle East under British or French control.

1922 Egypt declares independence. After short war, Kuwait and Saudi Arabia agree to shared frontier.

1927 Huge oil fields discovered in Iraq.

1932 Iraq gains independence. Oil discovered in Bahrain. Saudi Arabia founded from four tribal provinces.

1934–1938 Some of the largest oil deposits in the world are found in Kuwait.

1935 Persia's name changes to Iran.

1938 Oil discovered in Saudi Arabia.

1940 Oil discovered in Qatar.

1943 Lebanon becomes fully independent.

1944 After more than 1,000 years of foreign rule, Syria finally recognized as an independent republic.

1946 Jordan moves to full independence.

1947 Britain announces it is leaving Palestine. UN declares partition of the region into Jewish and Arab states. Fighting breaks out between Arabs and Jews.

1948 Israel declares itself independent, and neighboring Arab states invade.

1950 Bulk oil exports from Saudi Arabia begin.

1950s–1960s Money from oil makes Qatar wealthy.

1951 Independent Kingdom of Libya declared.

1956 Israel occupies Gaza Strip.

1958 Huge oil fields in Abu Dhabi (UAE) discovered.

1959 Oil and natural gas discovered in Libya.

1960s Disputes between Israel, Syria, and Jordan over use of the Jordan River's water.

1960–1970 Construction of Aswan High Dam in Egypt.

1961 Syria regains independence.

1964 Oil discovered in Oman. Palestine Liberation Organization (PLO) founded.

1967 Israel defeats Egypt, Syria, and Jordan and captures Gaza, the West Bank, East Jerusalem, and the Golan Heights (Syria) in the Six-Day War.

1971 Kuwait agrees on a new frontier with Saudi Arabia. Qatar and Bahrain become independent nations.

1971–1972 Seven emirates unite to form the United Arab Emirates.

1980 Oil discovered in Yemen.

1980s Turkish government starts constructing Ataturk Dam, which threatens to affect supplies of water to Syria and Iraq.

1980–1988 Iran-Iraq go to war over disputed borders.

1982–2000 Israel invades and occupies southern Lebanon.

1984 Great Man-Made River Project begins in Libya.

1990 Yemen becomes a unified state.

1993 Ancient city of Petra in Jordan designated a national park.

1994–1995 Palestinian National Authority founded.

1999 and 2003 Oman agrees on border treaties with United Arab Emirates.

2000 Natural gas discovered off the coast of Israel.

2002 Construction of the Israel's security wall begins.

GLOSSARY

alluvial soil: soil formed from deposits carried by rivers

aquifer: a body of underground water

Arabian peninsula: the large area of land surrounded on three sides by the Red Sea, Arabian Sea, and Persian Gulf

armaments: weapons and other military equipment

Bedouin: Arab nomad

biotech: short for biotechnology, the use of biological processes for industrial purposes

causeway: a raised road across water or low ground

colonial: having to do with one country controlling or settling in another country

coniferous: cone bearing

deciduous: shedding leaves in winter

desalination: the process of removing salt

emirate: a Middle Eastern kingdom, ruled by an emir

ethnic group: a group of people that shares tribal, cultural, linguistic, or racial characteristics

evaporate: to turn to vapor

exports: goods that are sent to other countries to be sold

Fertile Crescent: the wide area that stretches in a long curve from northern Israel, through Lebanon and Syria, and down through Iraq toward the Persian Gulf

fertile soil: soil rich in nutrients in which it is easy to grow crops

financial services: services such as banking, insurance, and investment advice

floodplains: the flat areas on either bank of a river

fuel minerals: minerals that can be burned to produce energy

gypsum: a mineral used to make plaster

hydroelectric power: electricity generated by the flow of water

immigrant worker: someone who comes from another country to work

irrigation: using man-made channels to move water from its source to agricultural land

Islam: one of the world's three major monotheistic (one God) religions (along with Christianity and Judaism), founded in the seventh century by the Prophet Muhammad

Islamic laws and customs: laws and customs that derive from Islamic holy texts and traditional practice in Islamic countries

Judaism: the oldest of the world's three major monotheistic (one God) religions (along with Christianity and Islam)

GLOSSARY

Kurds: a Middle Eastern people, mostly Sunni Muslims, who have no state of their own but form large minorities in Turkey, Iraq, and Iran

mandate territory: a territory in which one foreign power has been given the temporary right to rule

maritime: having to do with the sea

Maronite Christians: the most numerous of the Arab Christian groups in Lebanon

Mesopotamian provinces: the lowlands watered by the Tigris and Euphrates rivers during the time of the Ottoman Empire

monsoon rains: seasonal rains that affect the lands adjoining the Indian Ocean area

Muslims: followers of Islam

nomadic: not settled in one place

nomads: people who roam from place to place in search of fresh pasture for their animals

nonfuel minerals: minerals, such as iron, copper, or tin, that cannot be burned to produce energy

oasis: fertile place in a desert

Ottoman Empire: the empire of the Ottoman Turks, which lasted from 1299 to 1922, and which included all of the Middle East except Iran and the desert interior of the Arabian Peninsula

Palestine: the name of the region roughly bounded by the Mediterranean Sea, Negev Desert, Jordan River, and Syrian/Lebanese uplands. The British were given a mandate to rule this region after World War I, and it was partitioned between the Palestinian Jews and Palestinian Arabs after World War II by the United Nations. The Jewish state (Israel) was established in part of Palestine in 1948. The Arab state is still to be established.

pastoral: to do with the raising of flocks or herds of animals

pasture: land suitable for animal grazing

plateau: an area of fairly level high ground

proven reserves: reserves that are definitely known to be there

semitropical: partly within or bordering on the tropics

Silk Road: the overland routes connecting China, the Middle East, and Europe from the first century B.C. onward

sorghum: a type of cereal grass

steppe: a grassy plain

transportation infrastructure: a system of roads, railroads, shipping, and air routes

wadi: dry channel or valley caused by intermittent runoff of water

FURTHER RESOURCES

Websites

Columbia University Middle East Studies Internet Resources
www.columbia.edu/cu/lweb/indiv/mideast/cuvlm/
Middle East: Geography, Maps, and Information
www.geography.about.com/library/maps/blmideast.htm
Geography: An Ancient and Modern Crossroads
www.pbs.org/wgbh/globalconnections/mideast/themes/geography/
index.html

Note to educators and parents: The publisher has carefully reviewed these Web sites to ensure that they are suitable for children. Many Web sites change frequently, however, and Gareth Stevens, Inc., cannot guarantee that a site's future contents will continue to meet our high standards of quality and educational value. Be advised that children should be closely supervised whenever they access the Internet.

Books

Bowden, Rob and Roy Maconachie. *Cairo* (Great Cities of the World). World Almanac Library, 2005.

Bowden, Rob. *Jerusalem* (Great Cities of the World). World Almanac Library, 2005.

Woolf, Alex. *The Arab-Israeli Conflict* (Atlas of Conflicts). World Almanac Library, 2005.

ABOUT THE AUTHOR

David Downing has been writing books for adults and children about political, military, and cultural history for thirty years. He has written several books on the modern Middle East. He has lived in the United States and traveled extensively in Asia, Africa, and Latin America. He now resides in Britain.

ABOUT THE CONSULTANT

William Ochsenwald is Professor of History at Virginia Polytechnic Institute and State University. He is author of *The Middle East: A History*, a textbook now in its sixth edition. Professor Ochsenwald has also written many other books and articles dealing with the history of the Middle East.

INDEX

Page numbers in **bold** indicate illustrations.

48